Love

in SIGHTS

BIBLE STUDIES FOR GROWING
F A I T H

Robert A. Noblett

WIPF & STOCK · Eugene, Oregon

Wipf and Stock Publishers
199 W 8th Ave, Suite 3
Eugene, OR 97401

Love
By Noblett, Robert A.
Copyright©2006 Pilgrim Press
ISBN 13: 978-1-60899-223-2
Publication date 1/18/2010
Previously published by Pilgrim Press, 2006

Contents

Practical Suggestions for Bible Study

One of the wonderful things about the Bible (with all its stories and limits) is that it allows us to be interpreters. It is open to all as we bring our own experiences to it. Bible study does not need to be boring, nor should it be. The following suggestions might be helpful to those who will engage in Bible study:

1. Read the text from several different translations, versions, or paraphrases. Note the differences in the readings. Have several persons read the passage aloud.

2. Center yourself on the text. Get into the text by asking:

   a) What questions, images, thoughts, or feelings does this passage evoke in me?

   b) With what character do I identify in this passage? What is that particular character saying to me?

   c) What is the passage really saying? Don't be concerned with "did this really happen?" Rather, look more closely at what the passage means.

3. Get into the Scriptures by role playing or creating a drama about the passage — actually be the characters. You will discover that many of the passages can be written as plays, with or without narration. Be creative. It is not sacrilegious to explore ways to interpret the meanings of texts for us in this day and age, or extract personal meaning on our own religious and spiritual journeys. Let the Bible speak to you. Do not confine your thinking to how it has always been. Contemporize the event, characters, and message as much as possible. What does it mean or what could it mean for you today?

4. Use your imagination. Many Scripture passages can be interpreted in several different ways. Try to understand the themes, then "plug" them into your life and your faith experience. Examples: God's fairness, Jesus' inclusiveness and concern for the outcast, the lonely, and the fearful.

Introduction

If anything is consistently viewed as a panacea, it is love. What is the answer to the political conflagration in the Mideast? Love, of course. What is the answer to the alarmingly high divorce rate? Love is. How can we see our way out of all the "isms" that plague us? We can love our way out of them all. After a while, it sounds quite banal, and utterly meaningless. Yet there is no sidestepping the fact that love is very central to our faith. We regularly sing, preach, and teach about God's love in Jesus Christ, and the mandate that we love each other. So why is it that our love becomes tired?

I believe that in large measure "love fatigue" sets in when we forget love's translation into specific behaviors. Love is infinitely more than a good feeling, a temporary high. This is made exceptionally clear in Paul's celebrated articulation of love in 1 Corinthians 13. But even this beloved text has gone to sleep for many of us. We hear it read often at weddings and sometimes at funerals — Yet this can signal the real possibility that this treatise has become far too domesticated. It has an edge, but that edge can become dull. It has awesome power, but it can be the power of an automobile in neutral instead of in drive.

The stakes, though, are high. Before St. Paul gets into the nitty-gritty of what makes love love, he begins with a series of "if" statements. "If I speak in the tongues of mortals and of angels..." — he has the glib talkers in mind. "...if I have prophetic powers, and understand all mysteries and all knowledge..." — he has the erudite in mind. "If I give away all my possessions, and if I hand over my body so that I may boast..." — he has the technically correct in mind.

After cataloguing these three scenarios, Paul goes on to say that as fine and impressive as each is, if it is not love that does the motivating in each instance, nothing is accomplished. These exertions are empty. The glib talkers come off as noisy gongs and clanging cymbals; the intellectually accomplished are basically good for nothing; and the show-offs have gained nothing. Love is that central, Paul is saying.

So where lies the problem with love? Love, as we often try to understand it and practice it, has been cut off from its fundamental components. It's infinitely more than warm fuzzies and it marshals powers both emotive and cerebral.

When Timothy McVeigh was executed for the Oklahoma City bombing, the press coverage was overwhelming. But amid the Niagara of words, there was a news story about a man from Oklahoma City named Bud Welch. Mr. Welch's daughter was killed in the blast. In the wake of his loss, Bud Welch began drinking heavily and his pack-and-a-half cigarette habit doubled.

Understandably bitter, Mr. Welch said of McVeigh and Terry Nichols: "I just wanted them fried." This attitude continued for about a year until one day — hung over and standing near the bombing site — he determined to change.

Bud Welch remembered seeing Timothy McVeigh's father, Bill, being interviewed on television: "I could see quite a large man who was stooped in grief. I could see the pain in his eyes. I recognized the pain because I was going through it." Mr. Welch came to the conclusion that "there's no healing from killing people," and he began to travel around the country speaking against the death penalty and for forgiveness.

One day Welch was traveling in upstate New York and allowed a nun to arrange a visit with Bill McVeigh and his daughter, Jennifer. As the two men discussed McVeigh's garden, they found common ground. The two Irishmen had been raised Catholic.

In the McVeigh home, Welch couldn't take his eyes off a picture of Tim McVeigh. "I said, 'God, what a good-looking kid.'" A tear formed in Bill McVeigh's eye. Bud Welch later remarked: "What I found that morning in western New York was a bigger victim than myself."

Before leaving the McVeighs that day, Welch put his arms around Jennifer and said to her: "Honey, the three of us are in this for the rest of our lives."

Later that night Bud Welch sobbed: "It was like all of this tremendous weight had been removed from my shoulders. I never felt closer to God than I did at that moment."

Such is the work of love that Christians have preached, taught and sung about for centuries. Let's take an excursion to love by revisiting biblical highlights that shed light on its nature. We begin by looking at some baggage we may carry with us as we depart.

As We Depart
The Baggage We Carry
ROMANS 12: 9-13

Let love be genuine; hate what is evil, hold fast to what is good; love one another with mutual affection; outdo one another in showing honor. Do not lag in zeal, be ardent in spirit, serve the Lord. Rejoice in hope, be patient in suffering, persevere in prayer. Contribute to the needs of the saints, extend hospitality to strangers.

"Let love be genuine," admonishes St. Paul (vs.9). The implication is only too clear. Sometimes love is disingenuous. So as we begin our trip through the Bible, it is clear that we depart with lots of baggage regarding love. We need to identify our baggage. The baggage doesn't own us; we own it. In other words, we have carry-on luggage when it comes to love; therefore we need to take steps to make sure the carry-ons do not get between us and what the Bible wants to tell us about the dynamics of love. Let's identify some of that baggage so that it will not become lost within us and perhaps torpedo the Bible's efforts to tell us about the real thing.

Bag # 1: Love is primarily a feeling. We know we love someone else because we feel that love in our hearts.

It was Erick Fromm who wrote about the confusion people can experience between "falling" in love and being in love. Fromm said this:

If two people who have been strangers, as all of us are, suddenly let the wall between them break down and feel close, feel one, this moment of oneness is one of the most exhilarating, most exciting experiences in life...However, this type of love is by its very nature not lasting. The two persons become well acquainted, their intimacy loses more and more of its miraculous character, until their antagonism, their disappointments, their mutual boredom kill whatever is left of the initial excitement. (*The Art of Loving*, pp.3–4)

Healthy and good parents love their children, and hopefully they love those children wisely. The loving feelings that parents remember they had for their newborn infant never goes away. The feelings are always in their hearts. But ask the exasperated parents of a fourteen year old how they feel about their child who was picked up by the police after sneaking out of the house at 1:00 a.m., and now stands in the foyer of their home next to a policeman who has brought her back. I can guarantee you that they are not going to be feeling lovey-dovey. Sure they love their child, but their feelings at that time are not of the warm and fuzzy variety.

Bag #2: Love means you must like everybody. It was Will Rogers who said that he never met a man he didn't like. I wonder about that. Does what Rogers said relate to your experience? Some people are intrinsically likeable; others tend to evoke feelings of the opposite variety.

It is part of love's challenge that we love both the unlovely and the unlovable. Jesus goes right to the heart of the matter:

But I say to you, love your enemies and pray for those who persecute you, so that you may be children of your Father in heaven; for he makes his sun rise on the evil and on the good, and sends rain on the righteous and on the unrighteous. For if you love those who love you, what reward do you have? Do not even the tax collectors do the same? And if you greet only your brothers and sisters, what more are you doing than others? (Matthew 5: 44-47)

Some of our most rewarding exertions for love involve people with whom we would never elect to associate. In fact, it's not required that we hang out with them. So let's offer as one working definition of love the following: Doing what is just and caring and salutary with and for someone whom (were we not disciples of Jesus) we could easily forget about and go on our merry way.

Bag #3: Love means being a sap. That's the way a cynic talks. The world, as a cynic sees it, is pretty much full of people who are con artists. Therefore, to love other people is to place ourselves in a predicament where we will probably be duped. We, therefore, had better toughen up and side step such traps.

Some years ago, a lady came into my church and asked me for help. I asked her what she needed. "Money for food," was her response. At that time, I served a congregation where the church building was the site for a county run food program. It was almost mealtime when she came and so I said to her, "I've got just the answer for you. I can't give you money, but I can take you down the hall to a place where you can get a meal." With that she sort of snorted, turned on her heels, and left.

The cynic is partly right. There are people who are more than happy to con us — if we let them. But love parts company with the cynic at the point of strategy. We can still do the loving thing with people who are out to con us. Sometimes, it means saying no and yes at the same time. NO — to the con. YES — to the need. "I can't give you money, but I can take you down the hall to a place where you can get a meal."

Bag #4: Love means swallowing hard and doing something we would rather not. Up to a point that can be true. On a cold and snowy night when a sick neighbor asks if we would go to the pharmacy, obviously we would probably prefer not to go out, but love in that instance bids us do so.

On the other hand, there can be times when love means being passive; when love means waiting; when love means not responding. The greater portion of loving adolescents is waiting them out, and not being drawn in when we are baited. Sometimes the essence of loving is attentive listening.

In a Christmas television film titled, *The Gathering*, Ed Asner played a hard-headed businessman who is largely alienated from his wife and children. Asner's character and his wife separate, but after the passing of many years — and prompted by his terminal illness — there is a rapprochement of sorts. In confessing to one of his sons, Asner's character says of his wife, "She sat up here all these years waiting for me to grow up." Love often waits for other people to grow up.

Bag #5: Love skews our thinking. Finally, infatuation can do that, but solid thinking is an ally of love. When we love someone, that love is informed not only by the heart, but equally with the mind. That's why St. Paul encourages the Philippians by saying: "Let the same mind be in you that was in Christ Jesus..." (Phil 2:5)

In 1979, an ex-aerospace engineer and Zen Buddhist priest named Bernard Glassman established the Greystone Foundation in Yonkers, New York. When Glassman began his work in Yonkers, Yonkers had the highest per-capita homeless rate in the nation. Inspired by the Buddhist philosophy of "loving-kindness" (a Christian value as well), Glassman and his volunteers, using entrepreneurial skills, transformed that community. Former homeless people earned a living wage, participated in community life, and taught others marketable skills. What they have been able to do is a wonderful illustration of thoughtful love — love informed by the power of articulate minds.

On this excursion to love, we bring baggage, but reckoning with that baggage can help clear our minds. It can also ready us for what the Bible awaits to tell us about what St. Paul suggests is greater than either faith or hope.

Questions for Consideration and Discussion:

1. During your formative years, was the word love used much in your family? And if your parents and/or guardian told you that they loved you, what did that love look like in your mind?

2. How would you differentiate between falling in love and standing in love?

3. When you think of being loved by someone else, what are your expectations of that love?

4. Does love always have to involve affection?

A Stubborn Love

PSALM 136: 1-9

O give thanks to the Lord, for he is good,
*   for his steadfast love endures forever,*
O give thanks to the God of gods,
*   for his steadfast love endures forever.*
O give thanks to the Lord of lords,
*   for his steadfast love endures forever;*
who alone does great wonders,
*   for his steadfast love endures forever;*
who by understanding made the heavens,
*   for his steadfast love endures forever;*
who spread out the earth on the waters,
*   for his steadfast love endures forever;*
who made the great lights,
*   for his steadfast love endures forever;*
the sun to rule over the day,
*   for his steadfast love endures forever;*
the moon and stars to rule over the night,
*   for his steadfast love endures forever.*

There is a perception of long-standing that the God we meet in the Hebrew Bible is a God of wrath and vengeance, and there are some places where God is so portrayed. The story of the Great Flood in Genesis 6 is one case in point, and this divine declaration from Lamentations is another:

He has cut down in fierce anger
  all the might of Israel;
he has withdrawn his right hand from
  them
    in the face of the enemy;
he has burned like a flaming fire
  in Jacob,
consuming all around..
LAMENTATIONS 2: 3

It would be a huge mistake, though, to assume that such divine activities are the norm. Or to put it differently, it is not fair to the Hebrew Bible to only allow it to speak selectively. We need to hear the whole story.

Let's suppose that new neighbors moved in next to us and wanted to come over and introduce themselves. They saw us in our backyard talking with our son, and so therefore thought this would be an excellent opportunity to walk over. As they approached, it became clear to them that we were having a heated conversation with our son because he had behaved badly and angered us. So seeing what was going on, and sensing this was not the best time to introduce themselves, they quietly returned home. How tragic it would be if those neighbors never came back because they assumed that what they saw was all there was to see of us. In fact, most of the time the picture is very different.

It is precisely the same with the Hebrew Bible and its presentation of God. It isn't just one picture that is presented; it is a collage. And the dominant theme of the collage is not that of a vengeful, vindictive and vicious Creator; in fact, it is quite the opposite.

One strategy for offsetting this misperception is to re-familiarize ourselves with the book of Hosea. Read any essay about God's love in the Hebrew Bible and you will find a reference to this book. Basically the book casts God's relationship with us in terms of Hosea's relationship with Gomer; the latter is a mirror of the former.

At the behest of God, Hosea marries a whore. "Go, take for yourself a wife of whoredom and have children of whoredom, for the land commits great whoredom by forsaking the Lord" (1:2). Despite Gomer's election by Hosea, her wanton ways continue. Again, Hosea hears God say: "Go, love a woman who has a lover and is an adulteress, just as the Lord loves the people of Israel, though they turn to other gods and love raisin cakes" (3:1). So Hosea buys her for fifteen shekels of silver, a homer of barley, and a measure of wine. And he says to her: "You must remain as mine for many days; you shall not play the whore, you shall not have intercourse with a man, nor I with you" (3:3).

Scholars have debated the historicity of this account, but we miss the nub of this wonderful book if we do not understand that for the first time in the Hebrew Bible, it expresses the remarkable love of God for God's people in very intimate terms. It is through and through a love story, a story of God's reclaiming and repristinating affection. God's people are recalcitrant, defiant, and refractory; they are as Gomer is toward Hosea. But throughout all that, God is stubbornly loving. God is waiting for the day when love will win out.

The zenith of the story comes in the eleventh chapter. The depth of God's love is beautifully and movingly expressed:

When Israel was a child, I loved him,
   and out of Egypt I called my son.
The more I called them,
   the more they went from me;
they kept sacrificing to the Baals,
   and offering incense to idols.

Yet it was I who taught Ephraim to walk,
    I took them up in my arms;
but they did not know that I healed them.
    I led them with cords of human kindness,
with bands of love.
    I was to them like those
who lift infants to their cheeks.
    I bent down to them and fed them.

(HOSEA 11:1-4)

Another strategy for offsetting this misperception is to understand that God's anger is the underside of God's love. Indifference, not anger, is the opposite of love. So when we read about the kindling of God's anger, we are hearing about a love aroused anger.

I suspect that when we get upset because another person is angry with us, what most concerns us is that the other person will (in one fashion or another) walk out of our lives; they might, we fear, leave us physically, or at least emotionally. Imagine then how much greater the stakes when we feel that God might walk out of our lives. Where then would we be left?

In the Old Testament, there is a juxtaposing of God's anger and God's love, and that is because they go hand in hand. At the end of the thirtieth chapter of Jeremiah, this divine sentiment:

Look, the storm of the Lord!
    Wrath has gone forth,
A whirling tempest;
    it will burst upon the head of the wicked.
The fierce anger of the Lord will
    not turn back
until he has executed and accomplished
    the intents of his mind.
In the latter days you will understand this.

(JEREMIAH 30:23-24)

Then notice the opening sentiments of the very next chapter:

At that time, says the Lord,
I will be the God of all the families of
Israel, and they shall be my people.
Thus says the Lord:
The people who survived the sword
    found grace in the wilderness;
when Israel sought for rest,
    the Lord appeared to him from far away.
I have loved you with an everlasting love;
    therefore I have continued my faithfulness to you.
Again I will build you, and you shall be built...

                      (JEREMIAH 31:1-4)

Finally, we can also take full note of a phrase we encounter again and again in the Old Testament: God's *steadfast love*. It is found, for example, in the 136th Psalm no fewer than 26 times! Synonyms for this word include: adamant, inexorable, obdurate, relentless, single-minded, unbending and unyielding. Picture each of these modifying the love of God. This love is a love that pursues us unrelentlessly until it finds us; it is wholly active and engaged.

When we search for a metaphor reflective of steadfastness, we usually think of something immovable, such as a rock. But I have something very different in mind. Years back I used to drive from Carbondale, Illinois to St. Louis with great frequency. One day, driving along Rt. 40, I saw a plastic bag (the kind used to bag groceries) clinging to a wire fence; it was obviously deposited there by the wind. On the one hand, the bag was so vulnerable, and shaped by the forces acting upon it. On the other hand, it was so persistent and tenacious. Having found a home in that fence, it was not about to leave. I know this was the case because, on several subsequent trips to St. Louis, I would

spy that plastic bag still here, holding on, holding out —
day after day, night after night, in all kinds of weather.

I suggest that the steadfast love of God looks like that.
Clearly the love of God is affected- pained- by the foolish-
ness and folly of God's children; God's love is vulnerable to
such. But it is a love that perseveres and persists, hangs on
and hangs in. A stubborn love indeed, and a love that pre-
figures the love we sing about against the backdrop of the
New Testament:

O love that wilt not let me go,
I rest my weary soul in Thee;
I give Thee back the life I owe,
That in thine ocean depths its flower
May richer, fuller be.

Questions for consideration and discussion:

1. In your formative years, which did you hear more
   about: God's anger or God's love?

2. If you heard more about God's anger, who or what
   introduced you to God's love?

3. If you are still focused on God's anger, why might
   God's love seem so distant?

4. Can you recall a time in your life when your love for
   another manifested itself in anger? Put differently,
   do you remember a time when you became angry
   because you cared?

A Suffering Love

LUKE 6: 32-36

If you love those who love you, what credit is that to you? For even sinners love those who love them. If you do good to those who do good to you, what credit is that to you? For even sinners do the same. If you lend to those from whom you hope to receive, what credit is that to you? Even sinners lend to sinners, to receive as much again. But love your enemies, do good, and lend, expecting nothing in return. Your reward will be great and you will be children of the Most High; for he is kind to the ungrateful and the wicked. Be merciful just as your Father is merciful.

There is no such thing as painless love. To talk about painless love makes about as much sense as talking about dry water or low heights. Simon Weil put it in an interesting way:

Each time we have some pain to go through, we can say to ourselves quite truly that it is the universe, the order and the beauty of the world and the obedience of creation to God that are entering our body. After that how can we fail to bless with tenderest gratitude the Love that sent us this gift?

This is a quality of love that Jesus — through both what he says and what he does — makes abundantly clear. He dismisses a mutuality of affection as a labor of love because a naturally reciprocal love is easily achieved: "If you love those who love you, what credit is that to you?" Certainly that experience is a wonderful one, but it is infinitely more gift than labor.

Loving the unlovable, or the cantankerous, or the mean-spirited, or the indifferent, or the despicable is quite a different matter. That's what separates the children from the adults.

Call to mind that person you continue to loathe; that person in the past who hurt you, or someone you loved deeply. Understandably, we portray such people in the harshest of ways. We view them as all bad; rotten through to the core. Now hear Jesus say that we are to love them (not like them). What might that look like and feel like? Most would say it would make us look like utter fools, and so far as how it feels is concerned, revolting would be a good place to start. In all honesty, what we would like to do to such people is retaliate in kind, and make them feel as lousy and as full of hurt as they have made us feel. Perhaps from the beginning, loving such people has to do minimally with successfully resisting the desire to behave toward them as they have behaved toward us. And to do that is to do a lot — maybe more later? Maybe no more later?

This love to which Jesus summons us is a painful love.

It's also disruptive; it sets its recipients on their ears. They don't see it coming. It upsets their usual way of doing business. They are primed for one thing, and they get quite another. Sometimes it's more than a person can imagine.

This is so poignantly expressed in the musical *Les Miserables*. Javert, the policeman, has spent his life chasing Jean Valjean for a petty crime — the stealing of bread for a hungry niece. Javert sees life in black and white, while Valjean understands the meaning of grace. Late in the play, there is that point where Valjean has an opportunity to rid himself forever from Javert by killing him. Instead he does just the opposite. Not only does he not kill Javert, but frees him. This is more than Javert can understand.

Who is this man?

In a song, Javert wonders aloud about what kind of man Valjean is. Is he a devil of some kind? Why would he catch me in his trap and yet grant me my freedom? How can I allow myself to be indebted to a man whom I have relentlessly chased? Does this man not understand that his grace is my death sentence, that (as the song puts it) "granting me my life today, this man has killed me even so?" And with that, Javert takes his own life. It is, strange to say, a suicide born of loving kindness.

There are few things more powerful than this kind of love, so powerful in fact that some of its beneficiaries choose to turn away from it.

Painful and disruptive, this love. And now also decisive. That's why for the Christian community, the life, death and resurrection of Jesus Christ is so monumental. His life presents a new way of understanding the power of God, namely the power of absorbing evil and throwing back in evil's face its very opposite.

The author Kenneth Cauthen wrote a little volume he titled *The Triumph of Suffering Love*. In there, he recalls some lines from John Masefield's drama *The Trial of Jesus*. The dialogue is between Procula, the wife of Pilate, and the Roman centurion present at Jesus' crucifixion. Procula asks the centurion: "What do you think the man believed, centurion?" Comes the reply: "He believed that he was God, they say." Procula excitedly asks him: "What do you think of that claim?" The centurion side-steps and says: "If a man believes anything up to the point of dying on the cross for it, he will find others to believe it." But Pilate's wife persists: "Do you believe his claim?" Still unwilling to be forthright, the solder replies: "He was a fine young fellow, my lady, not past the middle age. And he was all alone and defied all the Jews and all the Romans, and when we had done with him he was a poor, broken-down thing, dead on the cross." Procula asks: "Do you think he is dead?" Now more forthcoming, he says: "No lady, I don't." "Then where is he?," asks Procula. The centurion then says, in a burst of affirmation, "Let loose in the world, lady, where neither Roman nor Jew can stop his truth."

The centerpiece of that truth is that love is stronger than all its adversaries, and the only resource that ever stops the cycle of violence.

And now a little postscript. This is not a scenario that finds the beneficiaries of this remarkable love winners, and us losers. Not at all. We win also, because we refuse to allow hatred dominion over our own souls. Ann Lamott is right when she quips that "not forgiving is like drinking rat poison and then waiting for the rat to die." (*Traveling Mercies*, p. 134).

And what of our national soul? William Sloan Coffin has wondered aloud about what might have happened if our national leadership had taken a different approach following 9/11, and said this:

"We will respond, but not in kind. We will not seek to avenge the death of innocent Americans by the death of innocent victims elsewhere; lest we become what we abhor. We refuse to ratchet up the cycle of violence that brings only ever more death, destruction and deprivation. What we will do is build coalitions with other nations. We will share intelligence, freeze assets and engaged in forceful extraditions of terrorists if internationally sanctioned. I promised to do all in my power to see justice done, but by the force of law only, never by the law of force."

George Briggs, an English cleric and poet from the nineteenth century, put it well:

I did not know the mystery of love,
The love that doth the fruitless branch remove;
The love that spares not e'en the fruitful tree,

But prunes, that it may yet more fruitful be.

I did not know the meaning of the Cross:
I counted it but bitterness and loss:
Till in Thy gracious discipline of pain
I found the loss I dreaded purest gain.

Questions for consideration and discussion:

1. Can you remember a time when your parents' love for you caused them pain?

2. Can you describe a time when your love for another caused you pain?

3. Is a painless love a shallow love?

4. What does a pained love say to the one loved?

An Engaged Love

1 CORINTHIANS 13: 4-7

Love is patient; love is kind; love is not envious or boastful or arrogant or rude. It does not insist on its own way; it is not irritable or resentful; it does not rejoice in wrongdoing, but rejoices in the truth. It bears all things, believes all things, hopes all things, endures all things.

Someone may tell you he is a consummate cook, but you can't be sure of that until he picks up the spatula and begins to stir. Similarly, one may tout the effectiveness of love in bettering the human condition, but you can't be sure of that until that person is active on behalf of love at those points where the rubber hits the road. A disengaged love is no love at all. Amazingly, Paul articulates the essence of an engaged love in just four verses from his celebrated description of love in 1 Corinthians 13. From those four verses, we can distill seven descriptors of an engaged love.

1. *An engaged love is patient.*

It was Catherine of Siena who described patience as "the very marrow of love." Patience is a great respecter of nature, and because patient love cooperates with nature, it is in sync with nature's timetable.

When we plant tulip bulbs in the fall, only the fool would try to insist that the bulbs, if rightly tweaked, could bloom in two weeks. Instead, we accept that the process is going to be several months in duration.

Loving other people, particularly the unlovable, requires that kind of patience. To wait patiently while they come to themselves, come to insight, come to conclusions, or even come to their senses — this is a manifestation of an engaged love.

2. *An engaged love is kind.*

When King Edward VII was Prince of Wales, he hosted a formal dinner designed to honor a man for many distinguished achievements. The man's table etiquette was none too stellar, and so when his tea was served, he poured some of it into his saucer to cool before drinking. Others around the table evidenced looks of mild surprise and wanted to guffaw, but the prince immediately poured some of his tea into his saucer and began to drink from it. Others in the royal party followed suit, and the guest of honor was saved from certain embarrassment. Maybe Alice Cary had this moment in mind when she wrote that there's "nothing so kingly as kindness."

3. *An engaged love is mannerly.*

Here's how Paul puts it: "...Love is not envious or boastful or arrogant or rude." Love is not green, not peevish, not prickly; not pompous.

There are some lines from George Bernard Shaw's Pygmalion that address this descriptor of love:

> The great secret, Eliza, is not having bad manners or good manners or any other particular sort of manners, but having the same manner for all human souls: in short, behaving as if you were in Heaven, where there are not third-class carriages, and one soul is as good as another.

I well remember a man in a congregation I served long ago who was abrupt, loud-mouthed, arbitrary and raw. Ironically his nickname was "grease." Manners are intended to grease the machinery of human interaction; they too reflect the loving spirit.

4. *An engaged love is freeing.*

Here is Paul: love "does not insist on its own way..." Love has no connection to that style of being with another we describe as "my way or the highway."

My wife's paternal grandfather, George Earl, was (by all accounts) a cheerful man. When Bob (my wife's father) was a young man, George took Bob on a trip to New York City. George asked what his son wanted to see in the city and Bob told him. George then asked his son, "How are we going to get there?" So Bob got out the map and developed a plan. At one point, so the story goes, they got onto a subway line that George knew was not the right one, but he said nothing to his son. After a time, Bob realized they were not headed in the right direction. George then asked, "Well, how are we going to get there from here?" Bob made revisions, and eventually the day's goals were realized.

My wife's father always remembered that as a treasured time with his dad. A father opened a wide variety of doors for a son, but did not insist that the son walk through any particular one. Rather, he allowed his son to learn through a process of failure and success; often the road to success is first the road to failure. George's love for his son was not a love that insisted on its own way.

5. *An engaged love is also even-tempered:*

"...It is not irritable or resentful...," says Paul.

When I was an associate minister, I used to get my haircut at a barbershop right next to the church. I did it largely for political reasons; I thought it important to have good relations with our neighbors. Bill was the barber, and he could be quite likeable. On the other hand, Bill could easily explode. One never knew what might set him off. One day I thought the cutting was going quite well, but something I said triggered him and he was off on a tirade about kids. I can still see his hands flying excitedly through the air (one of them holding the razor) with Bill plaintively asking in his German-charged English, "You know vats wrong vis children today?!!" I could never totally relax in Bill's barber chair.

By contrast, an engaged love is a steady-as-you-go love. Consistency is a manifestation of caring. This love's heart is large and absorbent, not dangerous and devouring.

6. *An engaged love is congratulatory.*

Paul writes that love "does not rejoice in wrongdoing, but rejoices in the truth." Said differently, love does not play the "gottcha" game. Love is not a competition; as though what we seek is in short supply, and can only be obtained when we win and someone else loses. The New English Bible renders it: "Love keeps no score of wrongs; does not gloat over other men's sins, but delights in the truth." Love does not traffic in the dynamics of the see-saw, where one can only be up when another is down. Love knows nothing of the put-down. And so much of television, and particularly so called "reality-television", is predicated on that dynamic.

I believe Claudia Rosett's observation is very much on target:

> It is no mystery why people sign up to appear on even the most revolting reality-TV programs. These shows are contests, and the contestants want the prize — whether money, fame or simply a chance to do something different. The more interesting question is why so many folks parked at home — with no chance of winning anything — choose to spend hours every week watching a TV genre that has evolved into a prime-time parade of greed, deceit and assorted forms of gross humiliation.

7. *An engaged love is benignly anticipatory.*

"It bears all things, believes all things, hopes all things, endures all things," writes Paul. Bearing, believing, hoping and enduring, all have a future reference.

On November 18, 1995, Itzhak Perlman, the eminent violinist, came on stage to give a concert at Avery Fisher Hall at Lincoln Center in New York City. Mr. Perlman, as you may know, had polio as a child and has braces on both his legs. He also walks with crutches. It is no mean matter for him to get to his chair, but he does it with grace and dignity. Once seated, he undoes the clasps on his legs, settles himself and signals the conductor that he is ready.

On this night, the ritual was as it always is, but something quickly went wrong. A few bars into the piece one of his violin strings broke. The break sounded like gunfire and there was no mistaking what had happened. People fully expected that he would have to painfully make his way off stage and either find another violin, or repair the broken string. He did neither.

Instead, he waited a moment, closed his eyes and then signaled the conductor to begin again. The orchestra began, and he played from where he had left off, and did so with passion, power, and purity.

Some would maintain it is impossible to play a symphonic piece with just three strings, but that night Perlman refused to believe that. He modulated, changed and recomposed as the music unfolded. It is said that at one point, it sounded like he was de-tuning the strings to get new sounds from them that they had never made before.

When he was done, there was only rapt silence — and then a deluge of cheers as people jumped to their feet and applauded. Perlman smiled, wiped the sweat from his brow, and raised his bow to quiet the audience. He then said, not boastfully, but in a quiet, reverent and pensive tone: , "You know, sometimes it is the artist's task to find out how much music you can still make with what you have left."

Anticipatory love is like that. It takes what it has to work with and — bearing, believing, hoping and enduring — it eventually wins.

Love has specific behaviors, and when they are present, love moves from being an abstract ideal to a present reality.

Questions for consideration and discussion:

1. Do you believe it is possible to love in general, but not in particular?

2. Can you identify seven people, each of whom exhibited a different Pauline descriptor of love?

3. What makes each of these people so memorable in your experience?

The Genius of Love

1 CORINTHIANS 13: 8-13

Love never ends. But as for prophecies, they will come to an end; as for tongues, they will cease; as for knowledge, it will come to an end. For we know only in part, and we prophesy only in part; but when the complete comes, the partial will come to an end. When I was a child, I spoke like a child. I thought like a child, I reasoned like a child; when I became an adult, I put an end to childish ways. For now we see in a mirror, dimly but then we will see face to face. Now I know only in part; then I will know fully, even as I have been fully known. And now faith, hope, and love abide, these three; and the greatest of these is love.

Having offered his counsel regarding what we have called an engaged love, Paul continues by lifting up the preeminence of love. "Love never ends," he declares. "Charity never faileth," is the way the King James Bible renders it.

Many years ago, the Army Corps of Engineers turned off Niagara Falls. Or to be more precise, a portion of the falls was turned off. This was made possible by diverting the constant flow of water to other portions of the falls. Nothing, though, was going to shut off Niagara's flow.

Paul is saying nothing will ultimately stop love's flow.

To buttress his case, Paul contrasts love with three other realities, and on balance says each has a life of its own, but it is a limited life. Interestingly, we try to give each of those realities a status each cannot, and should not, have.

"...As for prophecies, they will come to an end." Prophecy is the analytical eye of the church. It is the church, or individuals within the church, who eye the culture, then measure that culture against the values of faith, noting that often there is a wide discrepancy between the two. When we think of the prophetic ministry of the church, we think of people like Micah, Jeremiah, Hosea and Isaiah. Basically folks in this tradition bid for our attention and then announce, "There's something rotten in the body politic; common life is not as it should be; something is going on that is anathema to God; and there is a need for concrete change."

Certainly this is not an invitation to beat people up spiritually, but an invitation to do better because God wants us to do better — and people deserve better.

Issues, as Paul implies, come and go. Obviously, if not handled properly, they can divide people. If, on the other hand, they are handled properly, they can issue in growth for everyone.

Prophetic people can be people with edges. Unfortunately their message, as accurate and needed as it may be, can get lost because of that edge. I went to seminary in the late 60s. Some of you might remember the 1960s as a time of upheaval. Sound and needed insights regularly got lost because edgy people delivered them. During that time, I had a course in eighth century prophets that was taught by a man named Harrell Beck. One day Beck said something that has always stayed with me. Beck said, "We need to love people into judgment."

What Paul says here is strangely reminiscent of something Jesus also said. You may remember these comments from Matthew 7:

Not everyone who says to me, "Lord, Lord," will enter the kingdom of heaven, but only the one who does the will of my Father in heaven. On that day many will say to me, "Lord, Lord, did we not prophesy in your name, and cast out demons in your name, and do many deeds of power in your name?" Then I will declare to them, "I never knew you; go away from me, you evil-doers." (vv. 21-23)

We can deliver truth in the wrong way and end up contributing to the very evil we deplore. Truth telling is best delivered in an envelope marked "graciousness."

Issues come and go; people remain. And "speaking the truth in love" (Eph. 4:15) — remains the best and truest way to express whatever truth it is we have to express.

"...As for tongues, they will cease..."

Let tongues stand for the emotive dimension of faith. We ought to feel our faith, and both speak out with passion and sing with power. But feeling is not lasting. Feelings are like the wind — In some moments the wind moves with power, and in other moments the most delicate leaf hangs motionless.

American culture has a love affair with the "high" and this certainly has infected some segments of the religious community. Regularly we see videos of congregations where the music is played with power and people raise their hands to praise and worship God — and all that's fine, if that is one's preference. But the music can't last forever. Eventually the service will end, the drums will fall silent and all those worshipers will return to the more mundane tasks of life — commuting to work, caring for children, paying the bills, cleaning the house, weeding the garden, and caring for a neighbor or parent. The title of a recently published book puts it aptly: *After the Ecstasy, the Laundry*.

In a little parish where I once served, there was a physically challenged mother who lived with her physically challenged son. They did their level best to be there for each other. One daily task that was impossible for this mother was the act of putting on her stockings. Her son, of course, couldn't help. But everyday a neighbor came at the appointed hour and helped her with that task. After the ecstasy, the laundry.

Highs leave, but love doesn't; its genius is its constancy. Its expressions are often homely, but utterly satisfying.

"...As for knowledge, it will come to an end."

My wife's father worked in the telephone business for nearly forty years. If he were living today, he would be utterly mystified by fax machines and cell phones. What was cutting edge when he retired in 1974 is absolutely antique today. All this means is that knowledge is developing so rapidly that it is impossible to keep up with it. There comes a time when our knowledge ends. We live in a day when it is literally impossible to be a know-it-all. There are limits to what we can know.

The flowering of one's intellectual life is very important and helpful. Reading broadens and deepens us; it pushes back the corridors of our lives so they do not become too restrictive and provincial. But in the economy of God, knowledge is a gift to be employed, not an essence to be stockpiled. Knowledge devoid of purpose is like fuel in the underground tank of the gas station — if it doesn't get pumped into automobile gas tanks, what good is it? Alfred North Whitehead had it right: when he said, "The merely well-informed [person] is the most useless bore on God's earth."

Knowledge can make people go off in one of two directions. It can make them arrogant, or it can make them humble. Arrogance might be defined as emptiness not yet in touch with its need for love, and humility defined as love's open door. In either case, it is love — not knowledge — that carries the day. Or as Moffat puts it, it is love that never "disappears."

Prophecy, ecstasy and knowledge are limited and limiting human dimensions. They have their rightful place, but we dare not elevate them to the status of love because they cannot deliver as love delivers. In our childishness we may think they do, but in reality they do not.

When our need stands naked for all to see, it asks this question: , "Am I loved?" And, "By whom am I loved." Occasionally on cable television, you can see reruns of the once popular show, Kojak. Years ago Telly Savalas starred in the show and played the lead role of a detective named Kojak. Not infrequently, Kojak — lollipop in mouth — would ask someone, "Who loves ya', baby?" The church steps up to the plate and says: , "God loves you." This is a love that is unconditional in its bestowal, but clear in its demands. The author of 1 John minces no words: "Those who say, 'I love God,' and hate their brothers or sisters, are liars..." (1 John 4:20).

In our congregational families, we move in many directions simultaneously. We tend to matters logistical, practical, and mundane so much of the time, and those things we must do. But ultimately we are in the business of celebrating the love of God. And to the best of our abilities, we must use our lives as vessels for the deliverance of that love into the lives of others. That's why Samuel Miller, standing in a chapel redecorated in honor of his two sons who had fallen in World War II, said to those who had gathered, "There are only two things that matter in life, only two and no more, no less: love and death."

No one is a permanent member of this world. We are here for a time and the ultimate measure of our worth will be known by how little or how much we loved.

And please know there is a marvelous alchemy about love. When we are loved, it calls out the best in us and the best in others. Or, as Paul puts it, "Love never ends." It is continually about the process of birthing itself. That is our faith, and therein lies our hope.

Elizabeth Barrett Browning's words so beautifully capture love's continual sweep:

The face of all the world is changed, I think,
Since first I heard the footsteps of thy soul
Move still, oh, still, beside me; as they stole
Betwixt me and the dreadful outer brink
Of obvious death, where I who thought to sink
Was caught up into love and taught the whole
Of life in new rhythm.

Questions for Consideration and Discussion:

1. Could it be said that the continuation of the church — flawed though the church often is — represents the process of love birthing itself?

2. In what ways might the church retard the birthing of love?

3. Can you remember a time when doing the right or just thing was done in the wrong way, thus inhibiting the very love supposedly being enacted?

4. Can we view the resurrection as the ultimate expression of love birthing itself?